STEVEN MACKEY

PHYSICAL PROPERTY

for Electric Guitar and String Quartet

HENDON MUSIC
BOOSEY & HAWKES

First performed on July 14, 1992
Schleswig-Holstein Festival
Kronos Quartet with Steven Mackey

Recorded by Kronos Quartet and Steven Mackey on
Short Stories (Nonesuch 79310)

Recorded by Brentano Quartet and Steven Mackey on
String Theory (Albany TROY588)

COMPOSER'S NOTE

Physical Property is the third part of a trilogy for electric guitar and string quartet entitled *Fables with Three Tasks*. The mystery, microtones, and complicated narrative of the first two parts (*On the Verge* and *Troubadour Songs*) give way to a libido-driven romp in *Physical Property*. This music is about the energy of live performance.

Between the ages of eighteen and twenty, I was a professional freestyle skiier. My vision of perfection was to careen down the mountain, head over heels, arms and legs flailing, on-lookers gasping, and somehow end up at the bottom with a smile on my face and not a flake on me. This aesthetic comes out more in *Physical Property* than in any other work of mine. The piece demands that an unlikely combo, the quintessential classical music chamber ensemble and the symbol of adolescent rebellion, work together with consummate discipline in the service of joyous freedom.

– Steven Mackey

Duration: 16 minutes

PHYSICAL PROPERTY

STEVEN MACKEY
(1992)

Sharp, biting, rhythmic
♩ = 160

Electric Guitar
Violin I
Violin II
Viola
Violoncello

f pizz. *f* pizz. *f* *mp* pizz. *f* arco

7

13

f *mf* *f* *mp* arco *p* *f* *p* *mf* *mp* *f*

979-0-051-09846-0

First Printing 2020
Printed in USA

* hold the pick tightly with only the very tip revealed, causing the thumb to touch the string creating a harmonic; also known as "pinched harmonic"

33
muted
squeezed
muted
wild, exaggerated vib.
sul pont.
ff
wild, exaggerated vib.
sul pont.
ff
scratch tone
37
squeezed
41
ord.
add lower octave harmonizer if possible
(sul pont.)
vib. ord.
gliss.
fast gliss.
slow gliss.
gliss.
(sul pont.)
vib. ord.
gliss.
fast gliss.
slow gliss.
gliss.
flabby, awkward, not rhythmic

45
fast gliss.
slow gliss.
gliss.

49
fast gliss.
slow gliss.
gliss.

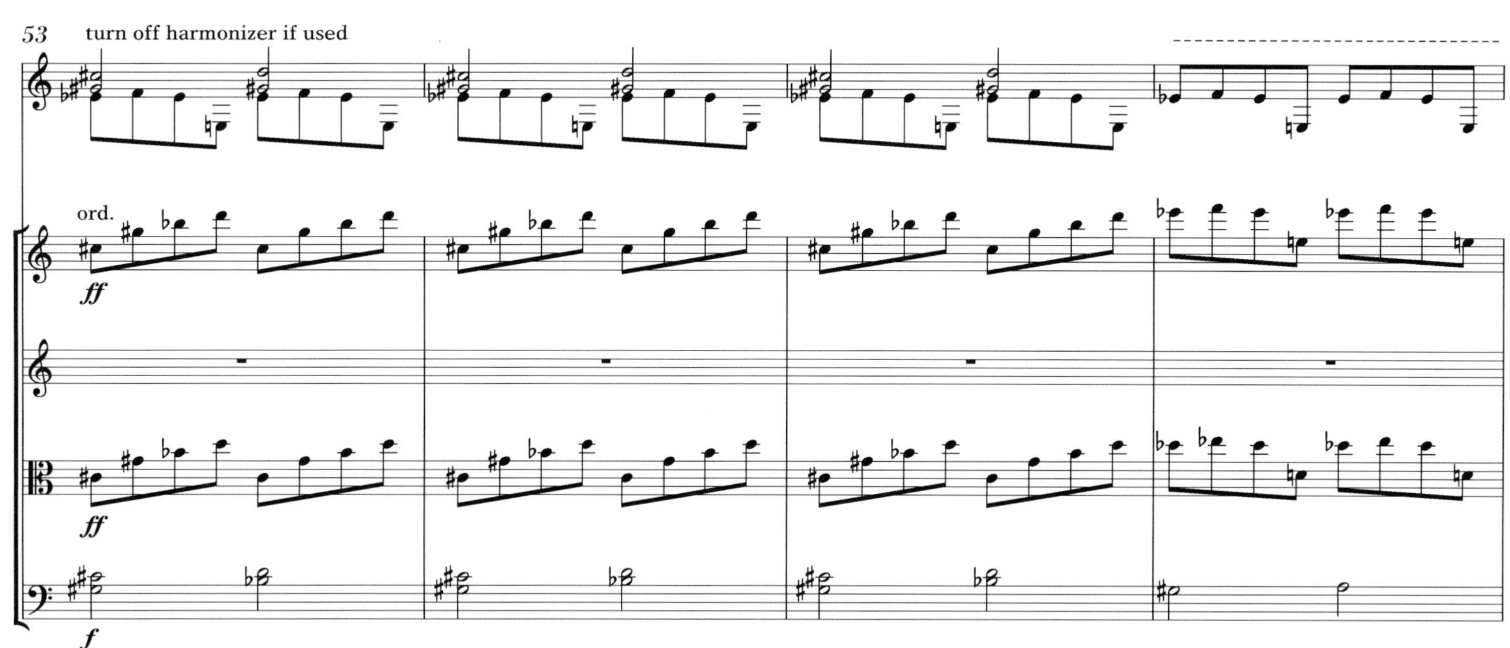
53
turn off harmonizer if used
ord.
ff
f

57
squeezed
ord.
gliss.
pp
p sub.
p sub., warm
61
ord.
p
p
p
p
66
mp
gliss.
mf joyous
mf
n
mf
n
mf
n
mf
mf
n
mf
n
mf
n

* Long, slow, free (rhythm), small (interval), legato, glissandi to be played throughout, as if it were an intense, mournful melody.

82
aggressive, rhythmically free
II
III
5:3
ff
f
as before: unison on II and III
5:3
3:2
mp
5:3
cresc.
gliss.
sim.
f
mp
cresc.
86
gliss.
5:3
ord.
f
gliss.
gliss.
gliss.
f
f
solo
gliss.
ff
91
3
gliss.
gliss.
gliss.
gliss.
ff

95
mf
f
gliss.
gliss.
gliss.
98
muted
ord.
gliss.
mp
f
mp
f
mp
f
mp
f
pizz.
mf
103
muted
mf
dim.
p
solo
non vib., rough
f
pont.
ord.
wide, slow exaggerated vib.
p
mf
dim.

108
non vib.
very slow gliss.
vib. ord.
113
ord.
pizz.
imitate Guitar low E thump
117
muted
[B]
long slow gliss.
sul pont.
long slow gliss.
(arco)
l.h. pizz.

122
126
2+3+2+2+3
ord.
3+2+2+2+3
mf joyous
f
130
mp
gliss.
cresc.
mp
cresc.
mf
n
p
f

* mournful gliss. melody, as before

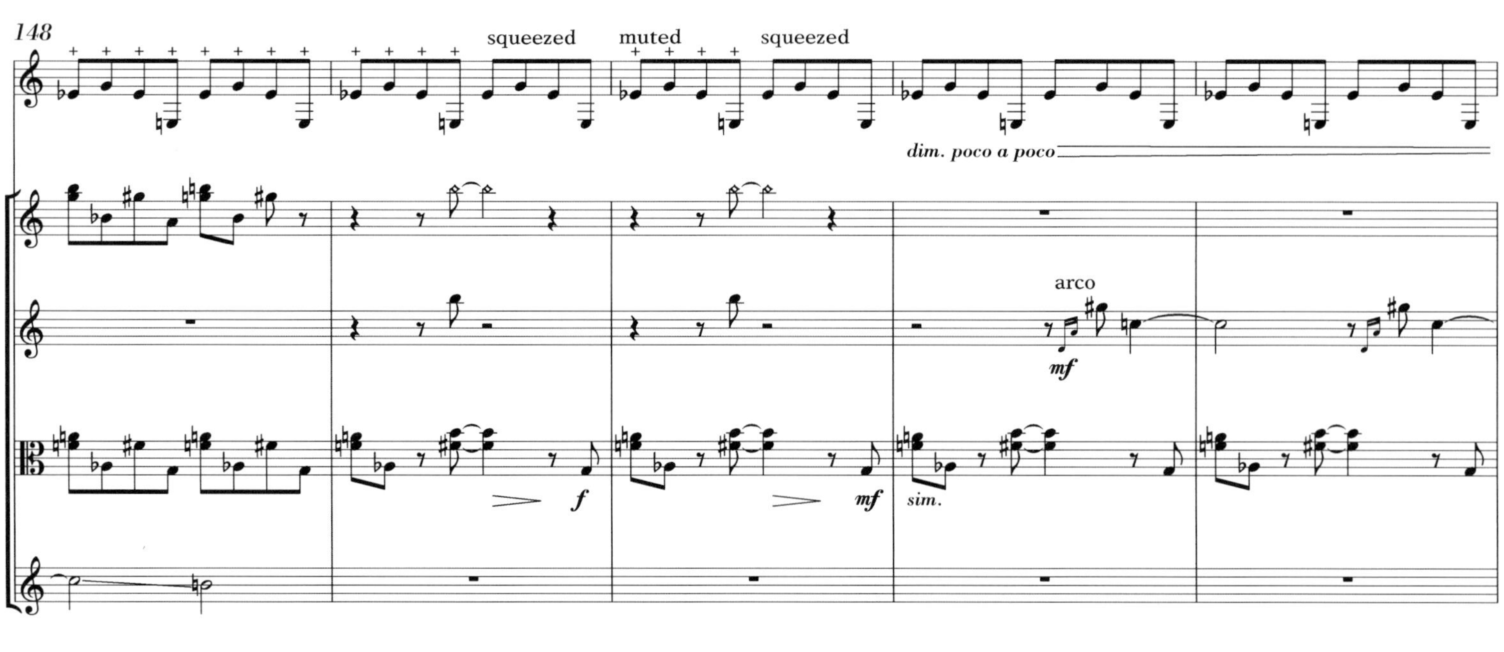
148
squeezed
muted
squeezed
dim. poco a poco
arco
mf
f
mf
sim.

153
improvised solo
n
gliss.
5:3
fp
bravura, flamboyant
ff
mf mechanical, restrained
3
f

158
(improvised solo)
gliss.
5:3
fp
bravura, flamboyant
ff
mf mechanical, restrained
3
ff
f

162
(improvised solo)
sim.
gliss.
5:3
fp
bravura, flamboyant
ff
mf
166
(improvised solo)
gliss.
fp
ff
f
170
(improvised solo)
5:3
ff
mf
gliss.
5:3
fp
ff

175
(improvised solo)
mf

180
(improvised solo)

185
solo continues but something changes;
maybe these notes are introduced
tr
gliss.
sul pont.
pizz.

190
suddenly in time and locked in
resume solo
gliss.
harm. gliss.
sul III
sul pont.
arco
195
(improvised solo)
petering out
pizz.
202
muted
ord.
romping, robust

207
muted
1st time
'scratch'
2nd time
210
ord.
f sub.
ff
gliss.
f
214
p
f
[A]

218

222

228

231
234
238
arco
sul pont.
thumb
gliss.
ord.
quasi-pizz.

241
bend
quasi-5/8
dim.
p
ff
arco
quasi-5/8
quasi-5/8
f
245
gliss.
mp
mf
n
249
8va
(or as fast as possible)
loco
gliss.

254
(8)
(tr)
gliss.
8va
f
6
gliss.
mf
p
p
mf
p
258
loco
p
f
3
6
pont.
f
p
f
gliss.
263
loco
mf
gliss.
p
f
gliss.
f

268
gliss.
[D]
bowed, on the string
poco pont.
273
ord.
sim.
276

280
ff
ord.
283
loco
mf
start slow
get fast
Not measured
free but fast
286
p

Not measured

288

(tr) stop trill

mp

freely, very fast; colla parte

mf

freely, very fast; colla parte

tr

(tr)

Measured; a tempo

289

no matter what, this is the downbeat

f

10

tr

f

stop trill

tr

stop trill

gliss.

f

293

f

298
mf
f
pizz.
arco
f-mp
302
306
p
mf
f

310
[A]
dim.
315
gliss.
f
p
arco
cresc.
pizz.
321
bend
mf
f
arco

325
arco
pizz.
pizz.
arco
329
p
arco
mf
pizz.
mf
pizz.
f
333
arco
dim.
dim.
mf
dim.

336
p
p
quasi-5/8
p
340
quasi-5/8
arco
p
p
pizz.
344
3
3
3
5
f heavy, harsh

348
352
357
arco
dim.
poco dim.

362
ff
ff
f
f
f
5
3
366
f
370
pizz.
gliss.

375
pizz.
pizz.
379
mf
ff
ff
arco
f
arco
f
arco
f
383
poco dim.
poco dim.

387
dim.
dim.
dim.
mp
392
rit.
(♩ = 126)
gliss.
gliss.
gliss.
gliss.
pp
n
p
Freely, a bit slower
397 ♩ = 104-116
f
gliss.
gliss.
gliss.
fp
f
pp
col legno

401
gliss.
a tempo ♩ = 160
404
bottleneck
gliss.
gliss.
gliss.
gliss.
ord.
407

* improvised bottleneck in manner of preceding but less tonally oriented, higher and more than a little bit crazy (finish between m416 and m418)

* pizz. ad lib.; pulsate on "sloppy" dotted eighths in fluctuating tempo
** pizz. ad lib.; pulsate on "sloppy" quarters in fluctuating tempo
*** improvised bottleneck (finish in m431); limit to following range: strings I, II and III at top and just off fretboard; a delicate, distant reminiscence of previous bottleneck
**** do not worry about exact sync. with Vn. 1—be lazy and change notes when you hear the Vn. change

432
wait for 6 pulsations of Vc. F
muted
mp
wait for 6 pulsations of Vc. F
pp
wait for 6 pulsations of Vc. F
pp
433
434

* Guitar wells up into an improvised frenzy moving up high, mostly noise.
Strings follow with a similarly chaotic improv. made of scratches, glissandi, and generally avoiding any strong sense of pitch.
The guitar calms down and returns to the lower register.
As soon as the guitar begins to calm the strings steer their own improv. back to the held B♭.
The guitar returns to the notated score around m. 449 and continues.

N.B. The guitar initiates both the chaos and the calming. The whole gesture "freak out and return" should take less than ten seconds.

454
2nd time dim.
p
non vib.
p
non vib.
p
459
solo
464
tr

468
472
476

480
tr
484
tr
tr
488